WHEN WE GET
CLOSE TO THE END–
SPRINT!

Unleashing Unused Retiree Vitality

BY
DALE E. YODER

Dale E. Yoder

Habakkuk 3: 17-18

ISBN: 1-4392-4407-3
ISBN-13: 9781439244074

Visit www.booksurge.com to order more copies

Scripture taken from the HOLY BIBLE, NEW INTERNATIONAL VER-
SION® Copyright© 1973, 1978, 1984 by International Bible Society.
Used by permission of Zondervan Publishing House. All Rights Reserved.

Francis, James Allen, One Solitary Life, Chicago, IL: Le Petit Oiseau Press,
1963.

Herman, Victor, Coming Out of the Ice: An Unexpected Life, New York,
NY: Harcourt Brace Jovanovich, 1979, ISBN 0151432880.

Powell, Paul W., The Complete Disciple, Wheaton, IL: Victor Books, 1982,
ISBN 0882073079.

Reprinted by Permission. Improving Your Serve, Swindoll, Charles
R., 1981, Thomas Nelson Inc., Nashville, TN. All rights reserved.
ISBN 0849902673.

DEDICATION

I dedicate this book to my wife, Nell, who is my critic, my confidant, my encourager, and my best friend; to my two wonderful children, Terry and Lori, who have overcome obstacles and yet remain faithful; and to my three grandchildren, Katie, Kellie, and Kyle and great granddaughter, Sophia, who bring joy into my life.

I pray the legacy I leave will help sustain them all through the struggles to attain success in their lives.

I give special appreciation to Lynn Petty, photography, to Paula Petty, design and to David Grall, for technical assistance.

Life is often compared to a marathon, but I think it is more like being a sprinter; long stretches of hard work punctuated by brief moments in which we are given the opportunity to perform at our best.

Michael Johnson
(400-meter world record holder)

Table of Contents

Preface   1

Introduction—   Out to Pasture?   3

Chapter 1—   Aging   7

Chapter 2—   The Brevity of Life   9

Chapter 3—   We Cannot Escape Death   13

Chapter 4—   The Necessity of Involvement   15

Chapter 5—   Setting an Example   19

Chapter 6—   Acting on the Word   23

Chapter 7—   Obeying the Gospel   29

Chapter 8—   Christian Virtues   33

Chapter 9—   Priorities   41

Chapter 10—   Wiles of the Devil   43

Chapter 11—   Appropriate Words   49

Chapter 12—   Our Reward   53

Chapter 13—   What Are We Supposed
                 to Do? Work!   57

Chapter 14—   Testimonials of Those
                 Who Sprinted to the End   59

Finis   66

Epilogue   67

Preface

You don't write because you want to
say something. You write because
you've got something to say.
F. Scott Fitzgerald

Retirees are sometimes treated like the old-time fire
engine horses. They are "put out to pasture," but when they
hear the alarm bell, their eyes flare and they whinny and stomp
the ground at the gate. Many still want to be in the arena but
have allowed others to take their place.

This book is written, not to place a guilt trip on us as
adults, but to point out our responsibilities while we have time
and opportunity. The time is coming when we age to the point,
mentally and physically, that we are no longer competent to
carry out the Lord's commands. At that point, if we have lived
obedient, humble lives of service, we can look forward to our
reward. I take it on faith that the readers of this book already
believe the Bible is the infallible Word of God and on that basis
make the observations contained within this manuscript.

I do not hold a doctorate in philosophy, but I don't have
to be a college professor to observe and record lessons I have

learned in life. I'm like one beggar telling another beggar where there is bread. Many people get their philosophy of life from TV talk show hosts who spout generalities and inaccuracies to the applause of their audiences. I would rather get my information firsthand from the Word of God.

There is a scripture that comes to my mind repeatedly: "From everyone who has been given much, much will be demanded; and from the one who has been entrusted much, much more will be asked" (Luke 12:48). I have been given so much. I had godly parents who gave me a core of solid values. I was the first in my family to get a college education. I had a job to which I was able to contribute and in which I felt accomplished, and a boss who appreciated and complimented my work. I have a wife and children to whom I owe a debt of gratitude. In retirement, my wife and I belong to a group of Christians who work lovingly and diligently to carry out the Lord's commands. That being said, since I have been given so much, I know much is expected of me, and I must not betray that trust.

I've written this book for four reasons: (1) to glorify God, (2) to cause me to reexamine my beliefs and actions, (3) to share these sentiments with friends and family members who might otherwise feel uncomfortable listening to these heartfelt words in a one-to-one conversation, and (4) to share with people with whom I will probably never cross paths. Time is of the essence; I need to share my convictions now because I shall never pass this way again. To quote an Old Testament verse, "The king's business is urgent!" (I Samuel 21:8).

Introduction— Out to Pasture?

What is going on in our many retirement communities? For the most part, it is a social time centered around a clubhouse with personnel who cater to every whim and encourage pastimes, i.e. golf, bridge, parties, outings, and swimming. There is a social calendar that provides a diversion for every waking hour. Yes, they may include a "Sunday worship hour" when some local clergyman comes and delivers a watered-down, inoffensive, feel-good homily about inessential matters.

Is this why Jesus Christ went to the cross and died? After we've gone through our last few years living in this kind of wasteland, will Jesus say, "Well done," when we haven't done anything but indulge ourselves in self-absorbed activities? Can you image the Apostle Paul loafing in such a place?

On the other hand, if we find ourselves in such an adult atmosphere, it is not too late to get out of the constant entertainment mode and start living an active Christian life. We can serve as examples and role models showing Christian behavior and servanthood. This cloistered community could provide a wealth of opportunities to put into practice what our Lord commanded.

There are ample occasions to visit hospitals and nursing homes, prepare food for sick people, send encouraging cards, telephone lonely people, comfort the bereaved and, perhaps, provide transportation for the indigent to the doctor or grocery store. I would think in an adult community there would be several lonely widows and widowers who need a good friend.

As important as meeting physical needs are, the vastly more important concerns should be the spiritual needs of those around us. Physical concerns have temporal import; the spiritual, eternal consequences. The best thing we can do is to have evangelistic Bible studies and invite our neighbors to attend.

Realizing that people such as us who live in such a place are in their last few years, we need to redouble our efforts to "snatch them from the devil's grasp" before it is everlastingly too late. Expect the devil to have a clenched fist, using adversity, persecutions, and roadblocks, because he does not want you rescuing souls headed his way.

When we consider the brevity of earthly life and the vastness of everlasting, heavenly life, we are overwhelmed! Have you ever considered the length (eternity has no measurement) of eternity? Someone observed that if every thousand years a bird picks up one grain of sand from the shore of the Atlantic Ocean and deposits it on the Pacific shore, when all the sand has been moved, eternity would just be starting.

If we are in heaven, that will be grand, but if we're in hell, the blackness, pain, and isolation will be intolerable and continual. If you broach this subject in casual conversation, people want immediately to change the subject to sports, the weather or any other topic. We don't want to think about that scenario, but it is a concept that bears considering. It is a thought that leaves me so awestruck that I cannot get my mind around it.

I just know I don't want to be separated from God, and I want everyone else I know to be saved as well. As the Apostle Peter said, "...make your calling and election sure" (II Peter 1:10).

Realizing the rewards or consequences, "what kind of people ought we to be?" (II Peter 3:11).

Chapter 1— Aging

"Here is a test to see if your
mission on earth is complete;
if you are alive, it isn't."
Robert Bach

I am seventy-four years old. I have lived a lifetime of learn-
ing, succeeding, failing, and observing the human condition.
And before it is too late, I'd like to share a few things from my
experience. It seems only yesterday that I was a twenty-year-old
with my whole life before me. Becoming a septuagenarian was
something I read about or saw evidenced in a nursing home.
And now, here I am at that age. A few years ago, I glanced in
the mirror and saw my father; now I look in the mirror and see
my grandfather! A nap used to be a luxury; now it is a necessity.
Gray hair has replaced the black and my brisk walk has been
reduced to a stroll.

What does my age signify? It means, according to the actu-
ary tables, that I have 10.1 years of life remaining barring an
accident or catastrophic sickness. How will I spend it? What

am I going to do with these few remaining years? Should I spend them in self-indulgent pursuits?

How about you? Now is not the time to sit back, relax, and take it easy. As the racer gets close to the finish line, he or she sprints. And that is what we *must* do: sprint into the arms of Jesus. Regardless of age, we are on the precipice about to take that last, gigantic step common to man into eternity, prepared or unprepared. Heaven is a prepared place for a prepared people. Jesus said, "I go to prepare a place" (John 14:2; Matthew 25:34). We cannot live irresolutely and irreverently in this life and then expect to be ushered into the presence of God in the afterlife.

A runner sprinting to the finish line will lean forward and crane his or her neck forward to be the first to cross the finish line. Runners strain every muscle, concentrate every thought, and focus their vision as they hurl their bodies onward. We need to think of ourselves as being in a race that demands our utmost as we serve our Master. Olympic runners are in a race to obtain a prize that is fleeting; we run a race to "get a crown that will last forever" (I Corinthians 9:24-27). We do not get credit for starting the race; we get credit for *finishing the race!*

Chapter 2—
The Brevity of Life

"We never quite find out what kind
of persons we are on our Palm
Sundays; it is in Gethsemane
we discover how much
character we have."
Harry Emerson Fosdick

I remember as a younger man visiting the rural church where my in-laws attended. On the bulletin board was a poster of what looked like that of an old man shuffling across a dirty street in a major U.S. city. The caption under the picture read, "On his way to eternity." That image remains indelibly imprinted in my mind. I cannot but be reminded of people I see each day rushing here and there but, in their hustle, are "on their way to eternity."

What will our legacy be? Will our children and grandchildren remember us for our service to the Kingdom or as those retirees who shared their lives for a while and then departed this earth without having made an impact? I heard of a family discussing how they wanted to remember their father following his death. They finally agreed his favorite past time was bowling. Hence, on his tombstone they positioned a granite bowling ball. Can you imagine such a hollow memory?

My tombstone and that of my late wife, Nan, is inscribed with the scripture: "I have fought the good fight, I have finished the race, I have kept the faith. Now there is in store for me the crown of righteousness, which the Lord, the righteous Judge, will award to me on that day—and not only to me, but also to all who have longed for his appearing." (II Timothy 4:7-8). I pray I may live up to the challenge in those verses!

Making Our Lives Count

Most "modern" parents discourage their sons and daughters from planning missionary lives that may include destitution and isolation in some foreign field. Most parents want their children to attend prestigious colleges resulting in careers that provide a soft, comfortable living close to home.

At church one Sunday morning, I sat behind a group of teenagers. The sermon had little relevance to their lives. The minister's mundane presentation had no spark, no passion, no urgency, and no challenge. As soon as the service was over, the teens immediately began discussing what movie they were going to see that afternoon.

What a waste of talent! Teens, like adults, need to feel their lives count for something of value. Adversity molds our character. As a result, young adults should be challenged to share their faith (Jude 3). That same scripture tells Christians young and old to *contend* for the faith that was *entrusted* to them. This is the training ground. If they have been instructed to serve in their formative years, they will continue their service into adulthood.

Instead of entertaining young people with trips to amusement parks, pizza parties, and picnics, we need to challenge each with opportunities that enable them to experience the effects of sacrifice and persecution. I know this goes against the grain, but it will make them stronger and in the long run give them fulfilled lives and a glorious eternity. There is nothing wrong with providing young people with a good time, but if we are trying to keep them faithful with constant amusements, we are short sighted. We must give them more substance!

We older Christians need to serve as positive examples for young people. If we, who believe in God, do not step up and provide that strong, forceful, encouraging image of what it means to be God's man or woman, youngsters will find their heroes elsewhere. We do not necessarily need charismatic individuals but rather those men and women who rely on God. The human being that God wants is a humble but confident Christian warrior.

We are called to be lights and salt: the light of the world and the salt of the earth. These two ingredients supply sparkle and provide seasoning to a world needing both.

Chapter 3— We Cannot Escape Death

"Because I could not stop for
death, He kindly stopped for me;
The carriage held but just
ourselves and immortality."
—*Emily Dickinson*

Ask children what they want to be when they grow up, and they may tell you they want to be an astronaut or doctor. Asked "what then," they might say, "Grow up like my daddy and momma." Ask a teenager what they plan for their lives and they might reply, "Go to college, get a job, get married, and raise a family." If you continue to ask, "Then what?" they might say, "Retire and move to Florida." If you ask "then what" again, they will be at a loss for words. Most have not planned beyond the short, physical life. This is the most important phase, the last eternal phase, and they give it little consideration!

The young may die, but the old *must* die. I don't want to be morbid, but I feel compelled, as Scripture does, to emphasize our mortality.

Job 16:22 reads, "Only a few years will pass before I go on the journey of no return."

"Life is just a mist, a vapor that appears for awhile, and then vanishes" (James 4:14).

"For all men are like grass, and their glory is like the flowers of the field; the grass withers and the flowers fall, but the Word of the Lord stands forever" (I Peter 1:24).

We read in Psalm 90, verse 10, "The length of our days is seventy years—or eighty, if we have the strength; yet their span is but trouble and sorrow, and they quickly pass and we fly away." We never know the date of our death or when the end is approaching, but we can be assured it is coming.

There was a merchant in Baghdad who sent his servant to market to buy provisions. After a little while the servant came back, white and trembling, and said, "Master, just now when I was in the market place I was jostled by a woman in the crowd, and when I turned I saw it was Death that jostled me. She looked at me and made a threatening gesture; now, lend me your horse, and I will ride away from this city and avoid my fate. I will go to Samara and there death will not find me."

The merchant lent him his horse, and the servant mounted it; and he dug his spurs in its flanks and as fast as the horse could gallop he went. Then the merchant went down to the marketplace and saw Death standing in the crowd. He went to Death and said, "Why did you make a threatening gesture to my servant when you saw him this morning."

"That was not a threatening gesture," Death said, "It was only a start of surprise. I was astonished to see him in Bagdad, for I have an appointment with him tonight in Samarra."

(*W. Somerset Maugham*)

14

Chapter 4—
The Necessity of
Involvement

"Of all sad words of tongue or
pen, the saddest are these:
'It might have been.'"
—*John Greenleaf Whittier*

Scriptures reveal that older people are to instruct the young (Titus 2:3, 6). But ever since I can remember, I have heard older Christians say, "I've worked long enough. It's the young people's turn." I do not find a retirement age in the Bible for Christians. Thus, my premise: as we get closer to the end, we need to sprint!

I wonder what would have happened if Jesus, early church leaders, and Old Testament prophets had had the mindset of today's older Christians who want to shelve their responsibilities.

Joshua, after leading the people to the conquest of Canaan could have said, "Choose this day whom you will serve. As for me and my house, we've just about had it."

Jesus, facing crucifixion, could have said, "This cross is too heavy to bear; my cup is too difficult to complete." Where would that have left us?

The Apostle Paul could have said, "I've left these letters for you to observe and abide by. I have given you some good advice and I hope you can follow my instructions. However, I cannot take it anymore! I have been shipwrecked, beaten, left for dead, betrayed, stoned and left destitute. You may have the same experience. Good luck!"

Abraham could have replied to God's instruction, "What, leave my ancestral home and father, become a sojourner and go to a place I've never been? You must be kidding. I've got it pretty good here."

What if Priscilla and Aquila failed to take Apollos aside and teach him the Word more perfectly? They could have said, "Some of the church leaders should confront him. That's not our job. And besides, we're tired of having the church meet in our house. Let someone else do it."

In each case, these individuals started and completed the race.

Moses lived 120 years and finished the race (Deuteronomy 34:7).

Joshua lived 110 years and completed the race (Joshua 24:29).

Abraham lived 175 years and finished the race (Genesis 25:7).

Jesus lived to be approximately 33 years of age and finished the race given him. In his prayer to the Father, he said, "I have brought you glory on earth by completing the work you gave me to do" (John 17:4).

We do not know how old Paul was when he died, but he finished the race. He said, "Not that I have already obtained all this, or been made perfect, but I press on to take hold of that for which Christ Jesus took hold of me. Brothers, I do not consider myself yet to have taken hold of it. But one thing I do: Forgetting what is behind and straining toward what is ahead. I press on toward the goal to win the prize which God called me heavenward in Christ Jesus" (Philippians 3:12-16).

Based on these examples, older Christians should say, "I'll work alongside of the young, share my experience, and be an example in word and deed." How can older Christians teach the younger if they are not involved and following Christ's instructions? We all have a role to play, and since we are on life's stage for such a short time, we need to "make the most of our time because the days are evil" (Ephesians 5:16).

We don't want to get to the end of our lives only to regret we failed to get in the arena.

Chapter 5—
Setting an Example

"If the average church should suddenly take seriously the notion that every lay member, man or woman, is really a minister of Christ, we could have something of a revolution in a very short time."
—Elton Trueblood

As we age and retire, our roles change. No longer are we concerned about rearing a family or "earning a living." We have time to do the things that were previously unavailable because of time and financial constraints. We need to ponder and contemplate what we should be doing. We need to set priorities for what is left of our lives. We need to make sure the last few years have value beyond sitting in a rocking chair. We need to take time for God, for our fellow man, and for prayer and meditation.

Jesus used a harsh word when he called a certain man a fool. In the parable, a rich man had a prosperous and productive crop. Not having enough storage areas to contain the produce, he tore down his smaller barns and built bigger barns. Then the rich man said to himself, "You have plenty of good things laid up for many years. Take life easy; eat, drink and be merry." However, that very night his life was taken (Luke 12:13-21). Are we in that category? Have we worked and saved and now think we can sit back and enjoy the fruits of our labor? We do not want God to call us fools for planning our temporal existence while neglecting our spiritual well-being.

Matthew 25 points out that when the Son of Man returns and all the nations are gathered before Him, he will separate the sheep from the goats.

The ones on the right will be commended for their active service to those in need. They will be surprised when told they had served the Lord by feeding the hungry, providing drinks to the thirsty, entertaining strangers, clothing those in need, aiding the sick, and visiting those in prison. What will our excuse be for not having followed the Lord's commands? At that point, will it matter?

Jesus has given us work to do. He points out there are crowds of people needing to hear the gospel but too few who are willing to share the good news. "The harvest is plentiful but the workers are few. Ask the Lord of the harvest, therefore, to send out workers into his harvest field" (Matthew 9:35-38). Let's get busy! Hebrews 12:1-3 instructs us to "…run with perseverance the race marked out for us." We need to "press on to the goal" (Philippians 3:13).

We older Christians are really an untapped resource. We have the time and funds to make a difference. Maybe it is not too late to flex our spiritual muscles and put on the harness of good works. We have "dropped the ball," and the younger generation is growing up spiritually illiterate. What can we do to rectify that situation? We need to be out front, leading the charge so those who follow will have a route mapped out for them.

Perhaps we can find some encouragement to help our young people from the following poem, which you have probably heard before:

"The Builder"

An old man, going a lone highway
Came at the evening, cold and gray,
To a chasm, vast and deep and wide,
Through which was flowing a sullen tide.
The old man crossed in the twilight dim;
The sullen stream had no fears for him;
But he turned when safe on the other side
And built a bridge to span the tide.
"Old man," said a fellow pilgrim near,
"You are wasting strength with building here;
Your journey will end with the ending day;
You never again must pass this way;
You have crossed the chasm, deep and wide—
Why build you a bridge at the eventide?"
The builder lifted his old gray head:
"Good friend, in the path I have come," he said.
"There followed after me today
A youth whose feet must pass this way.
This chasm that has been naught to me
To that fair-haired youth may a pitfall be,
He, too, must cross in the twilight dim;
Good friend, I am building the bridge for him."
—*Will Allen Dromgoole*

Chapter 6—
Acting on the Word

"God will not shout. God has much
to say that we do not hear because
we are too busy and the noise levels
too high. He whispers in the deep.
Only those who stop long enough,
or who are stopped long enough,
hear the text of the message."
—*Gordon MacDonald*

The apostle James wrote, "Do not merely listen to the Word, and so deceive yourselves. Do what it says" (James 1:22).

John quoted Jesus in John 12:48, "There is a judge for the one who rejects me and does not accept my words; that very word which I spoke will condemn him at the last day."

How can we read these words and go in our willy-nilly ways, shrugging off the import of these imperatives?

People get involved in a lot of different, time-consuming activities. They may try to "save the planet," rescue pets, or eat only vegetables, all of which may be good causes but require the preponderance of their time, while the more important issues of saving oneself and others eternally goes unheeded and unfilled.

Although we are bombarded with the message that the planet is being destroyed by global warming, I have no fear this phenomenon will happen. God told Noah, "As long as the earth endures, seedtime and harvest, cold and heat, summer and winter, day and night will never cease" (Genesis 8:22). That has been my experience over the past seventy-four years, and I expect the same sequence to continue as God specified. Natural events will continue until God "pulls the plug," and only then will the world grind to a halt. This message will be pooh-poohed by unbelievers and who are, by their words and actions, disciples of the devil. I would rather be in the company of the Apostle Paul who was "not ashamed of the gospel" (Romans 1:16, I Corinthians 1:18, 15:2).

In his book *Improving Your Serve,* Charles Swindoll makes the following powerful analogy:

"To make the value of obedience just as practical as possible, let's play 'Let's Pretend.' Let's pretend that you work for me. In fact, you are my executive assistant in a company that is growing rapidly. I'm the owner and I am interested in expanding overseas. To pull this off, I make plans to travel abroad and stay there until a new branch office gets established. I make all the arrangements to take my family and move to Europe for six to eight months, and I have to leave you in charge of the busy stateside organization. I tell you that I will write you regularly and give you directions and instructions. I leave, and you stay.

Months pass. A flow of letters are mailed from Europe and received by you at the national headquarters. I spell out my expectations.

Finally I return. Soon after my arrival, I drive down to the office and I am stunned. Grass and weeds have grown high. A few windows along the street are broken. I walk into the receptionist's room. She is doing her nails, chewing gum, and listening to her favorite disco station. I look around and the wastebaskets are overflowing. The carpet hasn't been vacuumed for weeks, and nobody seems concerned that the owner has returned. I asked about your whereabouts and someone in the crowded lounge area points down the hall and yells, "I think he is down there." Disturbed, I move in that direction and bump into you as you are finishing a chess game with our sales manager. I ask you to step into my office, which has been temporarily turned into a television room for watching afternoon soap operas.

"What is the world is going on, man?"

"What do you mean, Chuck?"

"Well, look at this place! Didn't you get any of my letters?"

"Letters? Oh, yes! Sure! I got every one of them. As a matter of fact, Chuck, we have had a letter study every Friday night since you left. We have even divided the personnel into small groups to discuss many of the things you wrote. Some of the things were really interesting. You will be pleased to know that a few of us have actually committed to memory some of your sentences and paragraphs. One or two memorized an entire letter or two – Great stuff in those letters."

"OK. You got my letters. You studied them and mediated on them; discussed and even memorized them. But what did you do about them?"

"Do? We didn't do anything about them."

Does that sound familiar? When Jesus returns will he find us "with our lamps trimmed?" (Matthew 25:1-13).

Paul W. Powell, in *The Complete Disciple*, described this condition thus:

> "Many churches today remind me of a laboring crew trying to gather in a harvest while they sit in the tool shed. They go to the tool shed every Sunday and they study bigger and better methods of agriculture, sharpen their hoes, grease their tractors, and then get up and go home. Then they come back that night, study bigger and better methods of agriculture, sharpen their hoes, grease their tractors, and go home again. Then they come back Wednesday night, and again study bigger and better methods of agriculture, sharpen their hoes, grease their tractors, and get up and go home. They do this week in and week out, year in and year out, and nobody ever goes out into the fields to gather in the harvest."

If we are not sure what direction our last days should take, we may need to stop, pray, search our hearts, read the scriptures, consider our circumstances, and proceed slowly. There is a time when we need to pause long enough to determine what God wants us to do. If we are constantly bombarded with the noisy din and glare of the bright lights, we may miss what God is saying to us.

The psalmist said, "Be still, and know that I am God; I will be exalted among the nations, I will be exalted in the earth" (Psalm 46:10).

Jesus said, "If you love me, you will obey what I command" (John 14:15). And what is love? The Apostle Paul gave a good definition in I Corinthians 13. Each time the word *love* is used, the Word points out a companion characteristic. Note: Love is patient, love is kind, it does not envy, it does not boast, it is not rude, self-seeking, or easily angered; it keeps no record of wrongs and does not delight in evil; it always protects, always trusts, always hopes and always perseveres.

A fine thing to do is place your name in place of *love* and see how you stack up or what you need to do to remedy your attitude.

Chapter 7—
Obeying the Gospel

"Trust and obey, for there's no other
way to be happy in Jesus, but to
trust and obey."
—J. H. Sammis

One of the most important things we must do is to obey and share the gospel. Paul seemed to think the gospel important because he said, "Yet when I preach the gospel, I cannot boast for I am compelled to preach. Woe unto me if I do not preach the gospel!" (I Corinthians 9:16).

What is the gospel? Paul continued, "Now, brothers, I want to remind you of the gospel I preached to you, which you received and on which you have taken your stand. By this gospel you are saved, if you hold firmly to the word I preached to you. Otherwise you have believed in vain. For what I received I passed on to you as of first importance: that Christ died for our sins according to the Scriptures, that he was buried, that he was raised on the third day according to the scriptures..." (I Corinthians 15:1-4).

To obey the gospel we must hear the Word, believe it, repent of our sins, confess Jesus as Lord, and be immersed in water for the forgiveness of our sins (Acts 2:38). The Apostle Paul wrote, "Or don't you know that all of us who were baptized into Christ Jesus were baptized into his death? We were therefore buried with him through baptism into death in order that, just as Christ was raised from the dead through the glory of the Father, we too may live a new life" (Romans 6:3-4).

In regard to baptism, Jesus said, "I tell you the truth, no one can enter the kingdom of God unless he is born again" (John 3:3). Jesus, the master teacher, was baptized (Matthew 3:13-17; Luke 3:21). Someone said, "If you are born twice, you die once, but if you are born once you die twice."

Some may say that burial in baptism is not important. Consider the following narrative entitled "Close to, Round about, or Nearby":

One Sunday, the "minister" was giving a sermon on baptism, and in the course of his discourse, he was illustrating the fact that baptism should take place by sprinkling and not by immersion. He pointed out some instances in the Bible. He said that when John the Baptist baptized Jesus in the river Jordan, it didn't mean *in*—it meant close to, round about, or nearby. And again when it says in the Bible that Philip baptized the Eunuch in much water, it didn't mean in—it meant close to, round about or nearby.

After the service, a man came up to the minister and told him it was a great sermon, one of the best he had ever heard, and that it had cleared up a great many mysteries he had encountered in the Bible.

"For instance," he said, "the story about Jonah getting swallowed by the great fish has always bothered me. Now

I know that Jonah wasn't really in the fish, but close to, round about, or nearby, swimming in the water.

"Then there is the story about the three young Hebrew boys who were thrown into the furious furnace but were not burned. Now I see that they were not really in the fire, just close to, round about, or nearby, just keeping warm.

"But the hardest of all the stories for me to believe has always been the story of Daniel getting thrown into the lions' den. But now I see that they were not really in the lions' den, but close to, round about or nearby, just like at the zoo.

"The revealing of these mysteries has been a real comfort to me because I am a wicked man. Now I am gratified to know that I won't be in Hell, but close to, round about, or nearby. And next Sunday, I won't be in church, just close to, round about, or nearby. Thanks. You have really put my mind at ease."

There are people who reject obeying the gospel because they think the rite of baptism is demeaning. Humbling oneself, rejecting their old sinful life style and going into the baptistry to have their sins remitted is anathema to them. They believe this condition for obeying the gospel is a shameful requirement. This kind of thinking reminds me of Naaman, a commander of the king of Aram, mentioned in the Old Testament (II Kings 5:1-15). Naaman had leprosy. In order to have it cured, he was told to wash himself seven times in the river Jordan. He left enraged; he had expected to have some great, formal procedure performed on his behalf. In the end, his servants convinced him to obey what he considered a trivial ritual, and he was cured.

In the same way, people today want some awe-inspiring mode of salvation to take place. I do not know why the Lord made this simple requirement necessary for salvation, but I'm not going to pass it up because it is beneath what I consider my dignity.

Does that kind of reasoning sound like something people do to rationalize their behavior?

Chapter 8—
Christian Virtues

"Do all the good you can, by all the
means you can. In all the ways you
can. In all the places you can. At all
times you can. To all the people you
can. As long as ever you can."
—*John Wesley*

Humility

The Bible speaks a great deal about the need for Christians
to be humble. Above all other traits, except love, I think a spirit of humility is most pleasing to God. Christians are called
upon to be obedient, humble, contrite, and submissive. "God
opposes the proud but gives grace to the humble" (James 4:6).
"Humble yourselves before the Lord and He will lift you up"
(James 4:10; I Peter 5:6).

Contentment

By the time we reach retirement age, we should no longer feel the need to "have things." We do not need to keep up with our neighbors, and we have either succeeded or failed in obtaining whatever position in life we sought. Now we do not have to live up to anyone's expectations except for those God has outlined for us. We should have learned the difference between a "want" and a "need." If we have food and clothing, we should be satisfied (I Timothy 6:6-8).

The Apostle Paul conveyed the secret to contentment when he said, "Do not be anxious about anything, but in everything, by prayer and petition, with thanksgiving, present your requests to God. And the peace of God, which transcends all understanding, will guard your hearts and minds in Jesus Christ" (Philippians 4:6-7).

Jeremiah Burroughs writes, "Contentment is not by addition but by subtraction: seeking to add a thing will not bring contentment. Instead, subtracting from your desires until you are satisfied only with Christ brings contentment."

Confidence and Assurance

Prior to his death, Winston Churchill, the great British statesman, planned his funeral, which took place in Saint Paul's Cathedral in London, England.

Besides many of the great hymns of the church, he planned an elaborate liturgy. At his direction, a bugler, positioned high in dome on one side of the cathedral, played the sound of "Taps," the universal signal that the day is over. Immediately, on the opposite side of the dome, another bugler played the notes of "Reveille"—"It's time to get up. It's time to get up. It's time to get up in the morning."

That was Churchill's testimony, that at the end of history, the last note will not be "Taps," it will be "Reveille."

I also find the closing lines of "Thanatopsis" by William Cullen Bryant compelling on this topic:

"So live, that when thy summons comes to join
The innumerable caravan which moves
To that mysterious realm where each shall take
His chamber in the silent halls of death,
Thou go not, like the quarry-slave at night,
Scourged by his dungeon; but, sustain'd and soothed
By an unfaltering trust, approach thy grave,
Like one who wraps the drapery of his couch
About him, and lies down to pleasant dreams."

A few years ago, my wife and I went to California on vacation. While there, we went to the Forest Lawn Cemetery in Glendale to see some of the graves of notable movie stars. Inside the pavilion, inscribed on the walls were the following encouraging lines that coincide with Jesus' words recorded in John 14:2:

"Another Room"

No, not cold beneath the grasses,
Not close-walled within the tomb;
Rather, in our Father's mansion,
Living, in another room.

Living, like the one who loves me,
Like my child with cheeks abloom,
Out of sight, at desk or schoolbook,
Busy, in another room.

Nearer than the youth whose fortune
Beckons where the strange lands loom;
Just behind the hanging curtain,
Serving, in another room.

Shall I doubt my Father's mercy?
Shall I think of death as doom,
Or stepping o'er the threshold
To a bigger, brighter room?

Shall I blame my Father's wisdom?
Shall I sit enswathed in gloom,
When I know my loves are happy,
Waiting in another room?
Robert Freeman

As we near the end of life, we can rely on the same promises that Jesus' gave his disciples: "Do not let your hearts be troubled. Trust in God, trust also in me. In my Father's house are many rooms; if it were not so, I would have told you. And if I go and prepare a place for you, I will come back and take you to be with me that you also may be where I am. You know the place where I am going" (John 14:1-4).

Self-Control

Has our older generation failed to pass morals on to our offspring, and in so doing failed our nation? This world hungers for ethical behavior from those who govern. We are constantly disappointed by the actions or misdeeds of our political leaders.

A better world begins with me. I like the following poem emphasizing self-control:

"The Man in the Glass"

When you get what you want in your struggles for self
And the world makes you king for a day,
Just go to a mirror and look at yourself
And see what that man has to say.

For it isn't your father or mother or wife
Whose judgment upon which you must pass,
The fellow whose verdict counts most in your life
Is the one staring back from the glass.

Some people might think you're a straight-shooting chum
And call you a wonderful guy.
But the man in the glass says you're only a bum
If you can't look him straight in the eye.

He's the fellow to please, never mind all the rest
For he's with you clear to the end
And you've passed your most dangerous test
If the guy in the glass is your friend.

You may fool the whole world down the pathway of years
And get pats on the back as you pass
But your final reward will be heartaches and tears
If you've cheated the man in the glass.
Author Unknown

Patience

When I was a senior in high school, I developed a severe strep
infection that caused nephritis (inflammation of the kidneys).
I remember the doctor telling my parents, "You have a very
sick boy." Fortunately, penicillin had been recently developed,

and I got four shots daily in the hospital—two in the morning and two in the evening.

When I asked the doctor how long I would be there, he said, "Oh, a couple of weeks." I remember replying, "I can't be here that long; I have classes to attend in preparation for graduation." But I spent five weeks in the hospital and an extended time recuperating at home. My meals consisted of Jell-O and some nasty, pungent broth (to this day, when I catch a whiff of a certain type of broth, I feel nauseous). It was at this time I learned patience. When you are so sick that you're flat on your back, God gets your attention. I was ill, and there was nothing I could do but wait until the medications took effect and the illness waned.

I have witnessed older Christians with serious health concerns still working in the Kingdom. They may have slowed down physically, but spiritually they are going full-bore. We need to keep on-course and continue running. We may slow down and stop to smell the flowers, but our momentum must always be forward.

Love

I was in a fast food restaurant the other day and I saw a couple making love!

No, not the cheap, titillating, sex-obsessed Hollywood kind; it was the genuine thing. An older man got out of his car, retrieved a wheelchair from the trunk and then carefully helped a woman, who I assume was his wife, get into the chair and wheeled her into the establishment. After positioning her next to a table, he conferred with her regarding what she wanted to eat. After ordering and receiving their meal, the man hovered over her like a parent caring for a helpless child. He put condiments on her sandwich, arranged her napkin, and then sat down beside her.

Now that is a demonstration of sacrificial, caring love. That is the kind of love the world needs to see more, and is the kind that Jesus showed when he sacrificed himself for the human race.

Chapter 9— Priorities

> "The main thing is to keep the main thing the main thing."
> *Anonymous*

I heard a story about a woman who saved for a long time to take a trip abroad. (I cannot substantiate the veracity of this story, but it makes the point.) She especially wanted to see some of the great cathedrals of Europe. She was on one of those tours where you jump off the bus, take a picture, and jump back aboard before it heads to the next tourist stop.

At one cathedral, a docent met her group at the bus and, after a brief overview, escorted them onto the grounds. He showed them the statutory surrounding the building and pointed out the graves of the notable departed. He called their attention to the magnificent building with its immense spires. Inside the edifice, he directed their attention to the stained glass windows that depicted various Biblical scenes. He continued by telling the group the age of the building and how long it took to build.

Finally, he asked, "Are there any questions?"

The inquisitive woman held up her hand and asked, "Has anyone been saved here lately?"

The docent looked stunned. He scratched his head, rubbed his chin and then responded, "Would you repeat the question?"

She again said, "Has anyone been saved here lately?"

He finally responded, "I don't know. No one has ever asked that question."

Now there is a religious body that forgot or ignored its mission and the mission of Jesus!

Are we of that same mindset but in a less prominent arena? Have we neglected the mission for which Jesus came? Have we allowed our desire for preeminence to supersede our responsibilities? Jesus said he came "to seek and save the lost" (Luke 19:10), and somehow mankind has relegated that concept to the back burner while promoting non-essentials in its stead.

What would officials at the Olympics do if a long distance runner ran the course on streets other than the ones prescribed? Would he or she win and get a gold, silver or bronze medal? Of course not. To please God and receive our heavenly award, we must "compete according to the rules" (II Timothy 2:5).

Chapter 10—
Wiles of the Devil

Now the serpent was more crafty
than any of the wild animals the
Lord God had made. He said to the
woman, "Did God really say, 'You
must not eat from any tree in the
garden'?" (Genesis 3:1)

We older Christians, along with everyone else, need to put on the "whole armor of God so that we can stand against devil's schemes" (Ephesians 6:10-18).

Satan is described in the Bible as a liar and the father of liars (John 8:44). His way is the road of disappointment, despair, disillusionment, and doom. He promises good but produces only bad. He paints a rosy picture, but his way is a dead-end street, a blind alley that leads to death.

The devil has other appellations: roaring lion, (I Peter 5:8), angel of light, (II Corinthians 11:14), and "he goes to and fro (back and forth) roaming the earth" (Job 1:6-7). However, if we "resist the devil he will flee from us" (James 4:7).

On the other hand, God's way is truth and life. God does not pull punches! He tells us that life's highway has bumps and ruts but, if we persevere, leads to joy and bliss.

It may seem easier to jog on the devil's smooth thoroughfare, but it is a sham. Jesus tells us to "Enter through the narrow gate. For wide is the road that leads to destruction and many enter through it. But small is the gate and narrow the road that leads to life, and only a few find it" (Matthew 7:13-14). As you can see, it takes no effort to be swept along with the crowds on the broad road, but it takes energy, effort, and discipline to hunger and thirst for righteousness and seek God's way. It may mean struggling against the current of modern religiosity, but it is worthwhile to be obedient and follow the old paths.

Even those on the narrow way need to be wary because the devil will introduce a slippery slope, and those successfully traversing the narrow way may be seduced to enter the broad way. Remember, the devil is likened to a roaring lion (I Peter 5:8-9) and is seeking additional recruits. He already has most people on the broad way! He is looking for the unwary to devour. He interjects troubles, sorrows, and problems so the faint-hearted succumb and give up. Rust never sleeps, and neither does the devil.

One of the devil's best subterfuges is to keep Christians busy with non- essential activities. This is not to say that many of the things we do are inappropriate, but they can be too time-consuming. Young people are busy with school, MTV, electronic gadgets, and sports. Young adults are busy with careers, family affairs, and community events. Middle-aged people find themselves concerned about investments, business contacts, and golf. Older individuals spend their time with grandchildren, retirement activities, and discussing health concerns.

The following is a thought-provoking narrative that emphasizes Satan's subterfuge:

"The Devil's Convention"

Satan called a worldwide convention.

In his opening address to his evil angels, he said, "We can't keep Christians from going to church. We cannot keep them from reading their Bibles and knowing the truth.

"We cannot even keep them from forming an intimate, abiding relationship in Christ. If they gain that connection with Jesus, our power over them is broken. So let them go to their churches; let them have their conservative lifestyles, but steal their time, so they can't gain that relationship with Jesus Christ.

"This is what I want you to do, angels: distract them from gaining hold of their Savior and maintaining that vital connection throughout their day!"

"How shall we do this?" shouted the angels.

"Keep them busy in the non-essentials of life and invent innumerable schemes to occupy their minds," he answered. "Tempt them to spend, spend, spend, and borrow, borrow, borrow.

"Persuade their wives to go to work for long hours and their husbands to work six or seven days a week, ten to twelve hours a day, so they can afford their empty lifestyles. Keep them from spending time with their children. As their family fragments, soon their home will offer no escape from the pressures of work.

"Overstimulate their minds so they cannot hear that still, small voice. Entice them to play the radio or cassette player whenever they drive. Keep the TV, VCR, CDs, and their PCs going constantly in their homes, and see to it that every store and restaurant in the world plays non-religious music constantly. This will jam their minds and break that union with Christ.

"Fill the coffee tables with magazines with magazines and newspapers. Pound their minds with the news twenty-four hours a day. Invade their driving moments with billboards. Flood their mailboxes with junk mail, mail order catalogues, sweepstakes, and every kind of newsletter and promotional offering free products, services, and false hopes.

"Keep shapely, beautiful models and handsome young men on magazine covers so that husbands and wives will believe that external beauty is what is important, and they will become dissatisfied with their spouses. Ha! That will fragment those families quickly.

"Even in their recreation, let them be excessive. Have them return from their recreation exhausted, disquieted, and unprepared for the coming week. Do not let them go out in nature to reflect on God's wonders. Send them to amusement parks, sporting events, concerts, and movies instead.

"Keep them busy, busy, busy! And when they meet for spiritual fellowship, involve them in gossip and small talk so they will leave with troubled consciences and unsettled emotions.

"Go ahead, let them be involved in soul winning; but crowd their lives with so many good causes they have no time to seek power from Jesus. Soon they will be working in their own strength, sacrificing their health and family for the good of the cause.

"It will work! It will work!"

It was quite a convention. The evil angels went eagerly to their assignments causing Christians everywhere to get busier and more rushed, going here and there with their hectic schedules.

I guess the big question is, has the devil been successful with his scheme?

You be the judge!

Does *busy* mean: **B-eing U-nder S-atan's Y-oke?**

Author Unknown

For Mature Audiences Only

Another of the devil's approaches is to use the term, "For Mature Audiences Only." Have you noticed the number of times at the start of a movie or television program the warning, "May contain adult materials?" When I see that disclaimer, I immediately see a red flag. Children, of course, should not be exposed to some of the filth being aired or printed. But when I see that precaution, I think to myself if it is not good for minors, it cannot be good for me. Jesus said in order to get into the kingdom we have to become like children (Matthew 19:14). I want to live so that I please God. I do not want to seem hard-nosed, but if we expect to get to heaven, we must become like little children (Matthew 18:2-4).

Many people say, "I know the film or novel has some foul language but the plot is good and the characters are outstanding. I know the Lord's name is taken in vain, but there are redeeming qualities." I do not like to see, listen to, or read material that is sprinkled liberally with four-letter words and sinful situations. Yes, I may be an old fuddy duddy but I think authors and directors can get their point across without offending our God-given values. People do not think this kind of material influences them, but used over and over again it desensitizes them to the point they are no longer outraged.

Alexander Pope had it right in this observation:

Vice is a monster of so frightful mien,
As to be hated needs but to be seen;
Yet seen too oft, familiar with her face,
We first endure, then pity, then embrace.

When I think of the argument by good people that a film or book is fine despite irreverent language and content, I think about a good piece of candy taken from the gutter. (I will make this as graphic and repulsive as possible to show the comparison to repugnant films and books.) It is good candy, made by one of the best confectioners. It looks good and probably is very tasty. You can eat it and enjoy it, except for a few downsides. You retrieve it from the sewer. As you pick it up you notice it has some mucus on it, some feces, and hanging on it's sticky surface is a filthy hair. But it is good candy. Anyway, you wipe it off with the cuff of your shirtsleeve in preparation for eating. Would you pop it in your mouth? No? Yet we devour, with gusto, mind-damaging materials day after day.

There is a vast expanse of knowledge that teachers would like to share with their students. However, teachers must constantly refer to the lesson plans so as not to stray from the prescribed curriculum. There are many facts that are good to know, but they must be pared down to what a student *must* know! Likewise, Christians need to keep "first things first." We need to "fix our eyes on Jesus" (Hebrews 12:2).

Chapter 11—
Appropriate Words

"Let your conversation be always
full of grace, seasoned with salt, so
that you may know how to answer
every man." (Colossians 4:6).

I have heard it said, "A picture is worth a thousand words," and that is true. Contrariwise, one word can bring to mind a "million pictures." For example, take the word *mother*. Can you visualize all the scenes that bring back a happy memory? Perhaps you can see her as you sat on her lap and she read to you, soothed a scraped knee or a bruised ego, cooked your favorite meal, or encouraged you to do your best. Take most any word, and you can have the same memory experiences, whether good or bad.

Words are important. A well-used, appropriate word can encourage and stimulate, while a flippant, off-handed, and cruel word can pierce and destroy. We need to choose our words carefully because we will be judged by the careless words we use (Matthew 12:36).

I talked to a woman recently who told me she wrote an appreciation letter to an elder who had served his congregation faithfully for forty years. After receiving the communication, the elder confided that her letter was the first appreciative letter he received in his many years of service. Shame on that congregation! That story should stimulate us to let people of all stripes know, if it can be sincerely done, how much we are grateful for their contribution to us and others. Surely, there is something positive we can write to encourage others.

There is a story about a man who was noted for his orneriness. When he died, no one could or would say a good thing about him at his funeral. In the same town, a woman always known for having something good to say about everyone was queried as to whether she could relate something good about the man. She remembered the man kicked the dog, yelled at children, failed to pay his bills and growled at the mail carrier. She thought and thought. Finally, she said, "He was a good whistler."

The point is that we can always find something positive to say regardless of the negative circumstances. Remember what your parents taught you: "If you can't say something good about a person, say nothing at all."

How Important Are Words?

Jesus said, "The words I spoke are truth and they are light" (John 6:63). He also said, "My words will never pass away" (Matthew 24:35). The Apostle Paul warned, "Don't go beyond what is written" (I Corinthians 4:6). When Jesus was tempted by the devil after his forty days of fasting, he countered every appeal with "it is written" (Matthew 4:4, 4:7, 4:10). The writer of Hebrews tells us, "The Word of God is living and active and sharper than any double edged sword" (Hebrews 4:12).

One of the most revealing examples showing the importance of God's Word is the reading of the law. When Nehemiah read the Word, people stood in rapt attention "from daybreak till noon" (Nehemiah 8:8). Again the people stood and listened for "another quarter of a day" and spent "another quarter of the day in confession and worship" (Nehemiah 9:3).

Yet in our shallow, shortsighted, nonchalant attitudes and impatience, we complain if a worship service lasts longer than the usual prescribed limit. We would not chafe at the length of an athletic contest if it went into extra innings or ended in a tie. In fact, an overtime game adds excitement!

Chapter 12—
Our Reward

"Grow old along with me! The
best is yet to be, the last of life, for
which the first was made. Our times
are in His hand who saith, 'A whole
I planned, youth shows but half;
trust God: see all, nor be afraid!'"
—Robert Browning

Working for God has its rewards. Sometimes we stand
open-mouthed as we see a beautiful sunset or gaze at the Grand
Canyon. As breathtaking as some of God's creations are, the
Word tells us the best is before us. "No eye has seen, no ear has
heard or mind conceived what God has prepared for those who
love him" (II Corinthians 2:9).

"So do not throw away your confidence; it will be richly rewarded. You need to persevere so that when you have done the
will of God, you will receive what he has promised" (Hebrews
10:35-36).

Being a Christian and living by Christian principles makes life easier for us than for the non-believer. We can sleep well at night because we have clear consciences. If our spouse is a Christian, we do not have to worry about the sanctity of our marriage. If our families observe Christ's teachings, we do not need to be concerned about anger, jealousy, pettiness, and competition with their accompanying recriminations.

Blessings

When I was a boy on the farm, we had no indoor plumbing and no central heating, for that matter. That was no big deal. When you are raised that way, you take your circumstances for granted. But wouldn't I feel put upon if I had to live that way today?

All who live in the United States, no matter how poor, live far above most of the people in the third world. Even the poorest among us have a roof over our heads, a solid floor, running water, heat, and food. We cannot imagine not having these necessities of life.

In his book *Coming out of the Ice,* Victor Herman described his pitiful existence in Russia during the 1930s. Victor went with his family to Russia to help Henry Ford build an automobile plant. They went with high hopes but were disillusioned from the start. Victor describes the harrowing experiences he had when arrested and placed in prison for political reasons. He survived by catching and eating rats. When he was released from jail, he was sent to the coldest part of Russia where he made his livelihood by cutting and selling firewood. He met and married a local girl, and they lived in a chophouse that was bitterly cold. Soon they had a daughter named Svetlana, who begged her father to tell her stories to help her avoid thinking of the cold and lack of food. So Victor told her of America and the city from which he had emigrated:

"In America there is a beautiful city and it is called Detroit. There are buildings and houses and people with fine clothes, and it's always very warm there. There in Detroit, the people are always warm and they eat all the time, and you cannot believe all the wonderful food there is to eat."

"Two potatoes, Papa?" his daughter asked.

"Two potatoes, sweetheart? Oh my, they eat wonderful things—ice cream and cake and cookies and roast beef and all sorts of chops and..."

"Two potatoes, Papa?" Her small mind was not capable of grasping what it was like to have ample food.

"Yes, my sweetheart, two potatoes. In the city of Detroit, everyone has a second potato."

It was unimaginable. It was the outer limit of magic, as far as a fairytale dare go. Two potatoes. What could be more fantastic?

Victor finally got back to America with his family, but his father and mother died in Russia. All the rest of her life, Svetlana would wake in the night grasping for a bit of anything, her mind forever captured by the specter of a morning without food.

How thankful we should be to live in a land of plenty and being able to provide for our families. How blessed we are.

Chapter 13— What Are We Supposed to Do? Work!

"Then I heard a voice from heaven say, 'Write: Blessed are the dead who die in the Lord from now on.' 'Yes' says the Spirit, they will rest from their labor, for their deeds will follow them.'" (Revelation 14:13.)

Some say you cannot earn your way into heaven. That is correct, but you cannot enter there without working. We are saved by the gospel, and Jesus expects us to "follow in his steps." (1 Peter 2:21). Our good works do not save us. We are saved by grace, but we are saved to do good works (Ephesians 2:8-10).

The final judgment will consist of individuals being judged on their works. John the Apostle wrote, "And I saw the dead, great and small, standing before the throne and the books were opened. Another book was opened, which is the book of life. The dead were judged according to what they had done as recorded in the books. The sea gave up the dead that were in it, and death and Hades gave up the dead that were in them, and each person was judged according to what he had done as recorded in the books (Revelation 20:11-13).

"So neither he who plants nor he who waters is anything, but only God, who makes things grow. The man who plants and the man who waters have one purpose, and each will be rewarded according to his own labor. For we are God's fellow workers; you are God's field, God's building" (I Corinthians 3:7-9).

There will be no second chance to right the wrongs, accomplish the tasks given us to do in this life, or make remedial efforts for opportunities lost. The writer of Hebrews penned the following words: "Just as man is destined to die once and after that to face the judgment" (Hebrews 9:27). "Work, for the night is coming when no man can work" (John 9:4).

Solomon, the wisest man who ever lived, said, "Work is the gift of God" (Ecclesiastes 3:13, 3:22, 5:19).

The word "work" must be important because the Holy Spirit saw fit to have it mentioned 793 times in the Bible. Jesus is no shirker. He spent thirty-three years on this earth doing the will of his Father and did not stop working until He said, "It is finished" as he hung from the cross. And to this day he and the Father are working (John 5:17).

Isn't it great that we get to work for the best employer in and out of this world: the Lord of Lords and the King of Kings!

Chapter 14 — Testimonials of Those Who Sprinted to the End

The following are examples of those who dashed to the finish line. They are listed in no particular order. I have included contemporary, Biblical, and historical figures to show there are both past and present individuals who illustrate what it means to finish the race by sprinting across the finish line.

In addition to these, the writer of Hebrews, in chapter 11, lists a whole host of heroes of faith who sprinted to the end. "They did not love their lives so much as to shrink from death" (Revelation 12:11).

Nan

The first person I think of that sprinted to the finish line was my first wife, Nan. I do not think she ever tasted a cigarette or a drop of alcohol, yet she died as a result of cancer on her sixty-third birthday. To my knowledge, she never had an evil thought or said an obscene word.

I came up with many hare-brained ideas, but she always supported me in whatever endeavor I pursued. I can only remember her being angry with me three times: when I bought my dad's Ford after we'd just finished paying off our old car, the time I spent one hundred dollars for a name-brand lawnmower when comparable Sears models were selling for under forty, and once, in the middle of the night, when I failed to put down the toilet seat!

She read to our children and started teaching them Bible stories before they could walk and talk. I was usually working, getting an advanced degree or traveling to conferences. Nan gets all the credit for the success of our children.

However, one of her greatest attributes was her attention to the needs of others. She was an elementary school teacher for twenty-five years but found time to sew clothes, refinish furniture, visit nursing homes, and study her Bible.

When she contracted pancreatic cancer, she underwent two operations. The surgeon assured us he'd removed the encapsulated tumor and she would be fine. Her oncologist, being an older and wiser man, advised her to "take her pain medicine and live her life." She wore pain patches but did not give in to her ailment. About that time, I retired and we spent a winter in Florida, where we worked for the local church visiting the sick and having evangelistic studies.

Upon returning North in the spring, her friends were appalled that she was not taking chemotherapy treatments. After some persuading, she went to a second oncologist who assured her he had some "new" chemo that would be effective in her case. From that time, her quality of life deteriorated. She died in July.

Prior to her death, Nan would drive weekly to the inner city to the shabby house of a mentally handicapped woman and read to her from the Bible. The woman's language was so unclear that she could only converse through her two middle-school aged boys, who were able to interpret for her. My son and I told Nan repeatedly that she was wasting her time; the woman did not have the intellect to understand and, in her condition, she was okay with the Lord. However, Nan persisted. The greatest testimonial to Nan was at her funeral: this woman showed up and sat on the front row paying homage to Nan's memory!

Nan left this world sprinting.

The Thundering Legion

Two emperors, Constantine in the West and Licinius in the East, agreed to legalize Christianity in 320 AD. However, Licinius reneged and attempted to suppress Christianity, ordering all Roman soldiers to offer sacrifices to the Roman gods. In attempting to carry out orders of the emperor, the Roman governor issued an edict that any Roman soldier who failed to abide by the command would face death.

A group of forty Roman soldiers, named the Thundering Legion because of exploits in their earlier years, would not obey the order. They believed in a higher power and said, in effect, "Nothing you do will cause us to renounce our allegiance to Christ." This infuriated the governor, who ordered them to remove their armor and clothing and stand naked on a frozen lake until they recanted.

The soldiers were told if they agreed to make the sacrifices, they could return to their ranks and be forgiven. Fires were built on the shore with hot baths, blankets, and food to tempt the men to change their minds. However, the men began to pray, "O Lord, forty wrestlers have come forth to fight for Thee. Grant the forty wrestlers may gain the victory."

Daylight faded into night and the men, despite the bitter cold, continued to resist. One man, however, unable to endure the suffering any longer, returned to the shore. The thirty-nine men continued their vigil. A centurion on shore named Sempronius, witnessing the scenario, shouted, "I, too, am a Christian," and immediately threw off his armament and clothing and joined the suffering martyrs. Throughout the night, the men continued to shout encouragement to each other, "O Lord, forty wrestlers have come forth to fight for Thee. Grant that forty wrestlers may gain the victory."

Their prayer was answered. By morning, all had died of exposure, but their courageous example of "being faithful unto death" has encouraged countless others, who have faced similar consequences, to remain loyal to their deaths.

I do not know to what theology these soldiers adhered, but I know God is pleased with those who are not ashamed of Him and "sprint to the end."

Stephen, the First Christian Martyr

Stephen, "full of the Spirit and wisdom," (Acts 6:3) and "full of God's grace and power" (Acts 6:8), was arrested on trumped-up charges for having "spoken words of blasphemy against Moses and against God" (Acts 6:11).

Stephen was able to adequately defend himself against their charges (Acts 7) but in the end was martyred anyway. "But Stephen, full of the Holy Spirit, looked up to heaven and saw the glory of God, and Jesus standing at the right hand of God. 'Look,' he said, 'I see heaven open and the Son of Man standing at the right hand of God'" (Acts 7:55, 56). They stoned Stephen to death as he left this life sprinting.

I find it interesting that in the above scriptures, Jesus is mentioned two times as "standing." The only other place in the bible that shows Jesus standing is Revelation 3:20. Normally Jesus is depicted as "sitting" on the right hand of God. (See Matthew 19:28, John 1:18, Ephesians 1:20, Colossians 3:1, Hebrews 8:1, Hebrews 12:2, and Revelation 4:9.)

What import does the aforementioned information disclose to you? It may be just a consequence that Jesus is standing, but I like to think of his standing in one of two ways: either he is standing to see how Stephen will react to the situation in which he finds himself, or Jesus is standing to honor one of his children who is making the supreme sacrifice for his Lord. I like to think the latter.

What do you think?

The Apostle Paul

Here is a man who was a persecutor of Christians until he had an encounter with Jesus Christ that changed his life changed (Acts 9). Paul became one of the great defenders of the faith and wrote most of the letters contained in the New Testament. In Paul's ministry, he instructed fledgling churches how to follow in Jesus' steps.

In the course of Paul's evangelistic endeavors, he had many harrowing experiences. For the sake of the gospel, Paul was imprisoned repeatedly, severely flogged, continually exposed to death, stoned, shipwrecked, and endured dangers from the elements and from people. He labored, was cold and naked, and experienced sleeplessness, hunger, and thirst. Why? He was in a race "to get a crown that will last forever" (I Corinthians 9:24).

At the end of Paul's life, he was confident he would get the victor's crown. He said, "I have finished the race, I have kept the faith. Now there is in store for me the crown of righteousness, which the Lord, the righteous Judge, will award me on that day—and not only to me, but also to all who have loved his appearing" (II Timothy 4:7-8).

When reading about Paul's life and the passion he had for serving his Master, I do not think he needed to sprint across the finish line; he was going "all out" all his Christian life.

Jesus Christ

Jesus came to earth to do the will of his Father. "My food," said Jesus, "is to do the will of him who sent me and to finish his work" (John 4:34). "For I have come down from heaven not to do my will but to do the will of him who sent me" (John 6:38). Jesus spent approximately thirty-three years accomplishing what he set out to do.

When praying to his Father, Jesus said, "I have brought you glory on earth by completing the work you gave me to do" (John 17:4).

While hanging on the cross, Jesus acknowledged that his mission was accomplished when he said, "It is finished" (John 19:30).

Jesus is the ultimate sprinter: He gave it all.

The following narrative is an essay written by Dr. James Allan Francis.

"One Solitary Life"

Here is a man who was born in an obscure village, the child of a peasant woman. He grew up in another village. He worked in a carpenter shop until he was thirty. Then for three years he was an itinerant preacher. He never owned a home. He never wrote a book. He never held an office. He never had a family. He never went to college. He never put his foot inside a big city. He never traveled two hundred miles from the place he was born. He never did one of the things that usually accompany greatness. He had no credentials but himself.

While still a young man, the tide of popular opinion turned against him. His friends ran away. One of them denied him. He was turned over to his enemies. He went through the mockery of a trial. He was nailed upon a cross between two thieves. While he was dying his executioners gambled for the only piece of property he had on earth—his coat. When he was dead, he was laid in a borrowed grave through the pity of a friend.

Nineteen long centuries have come and gone, and today he is a centerpiece of the human race and leader of the column of progress. I am far within the mark when I say that all the armies that ever marched, all the navies that were ever built, all the parliaments that ever sat, and all the kings that ever reigned, put together, have not affected the life of man upon this earth as powerfully as has that one solitary life.

When praying to his Father, Jesus said, "I have brought you glory on earth by completing the work you gave me to do" (John 17:4).

FINIS

"Behold, I am coming soon! My reward is with me, and I will give to everyone according to what he has done" (Revelation 22:12).

In every phase of life, especially when we get close to the end, we need keep our eyes focused on Jesus, sprint, and anticipating the joy to come, be confident that the "toils of the road will seem like nothing."

Is the race worthwhile? You betcha!

EPILOGUE

Dale Yoder was reared on a farm in Ohio. After high school graduation, he went to the Detroit area and worked as a clerk-typist in an automobile frame factory. While visiting a newspaper composing room, he had the impulse to become a printer. After working at the trade for a couple of years, he applied to Harding College (now Harding University), was accepted, and used his printing skills at the college to pay his expenses.

After graduation in 1961, he taught in Cincinnati public high schools: first, industrial arts and vocational skills, and later, since his degree was in journalism and English, those classes as well. He received a master's of education from the University of Cincinnati in 1970 and left the classroom to supervise teachers in a suburban Cincinnati school district. After working thirty years in the educational field, he retired.

He has two children, three grandchildren and one great grandchild. Dale and his wife, Nell, are Sojourners, a group of mostly retired Christians who have motor homes and do voluntary evangelistic and physical work for small churches, Bible camps, children's homes, and colleges. They live in Chattanooga, Tennessee, and within their limitations and capabilities, are "sprinting."